the complete

swimming
breaststroke

learn, improve and fine-tune basic
breaststroke technique

fully illustrated with
practical exercises

mark young

E&L

A Catalogue record for this book is available from the British Library

ISBN 978-0-9570031-2-5

First published 2010 by Educate & Learn Publishing, Hertfordshire, UK
enquiries@educateandlearnpublishing.com

Graphics by Mark Young, courtesy of Poser V6.0

Design and typeset by Mark Young and Baines Design, Cuffley, UK

Published in association with swim-teach.com
www.swim-teach.com

Contents

breaststroke

Breaststroke is the oldest and slowest of the four swimming strokes. It is also the most inefficient of all strokes, which is what makes it the slowest. Propulsion from the arms and legs is a consecutive action that takes place under the water. A large frontal

resistance area is created as the heels draw up towards the seat and the breathing technique inclines the body position also increasing resistance. These are the main reasons that make this stroke inefficient and slow

This stroke is normally one of the first strokes to be taught, especially to adults, as the head and face is clear of the water,

giving the swimmer a greater perception of their whereabouts and their buoyancy. There are variations in the overall technique, ranging from a slow recreational style to a more precise competitive style. Body position should be as flat and streamlined as possible with an inclination from the head to the feet so that the leg kick recovery takes place under the water.

The leg kick as a whole should be a simultaneous and flowing action, providing the majority of the propulsion.

The arm action should also be simultaneous and flowing and overall provides the smallest propulsive phase of the four strokes.

The stroke action gives a natural body lift which gives the ideal breathing point with each stroke and a streamlined body position during the timing sequence of the arm and leg action is essential to capitalise on the propulsive phases of the stroke.

body position

The body position should be inclined slightly downwards from the head to the feet.

The body should be as flat and streamlined as possible with an inclination from the head to the feet so that the leg kick recovery takes place under the water.

Head movement should be kept to a minimum and the shoulders should remain level throughout the stroke.

Body position at a slight angle if the head is above the water surface

Direction of travel

Body position flatter and more streamlined during the glide phase when the face is submerged

The main aim should be good streamlining, however the underwater recovery movements of the arms and legs together with the lifting of the head to breathe, all compromise the overall body position. In order to reduce resistance created by these movements, as the propulsive phase of an arm pull or leg kick takes place, the opposite end of the body remains still and streamlined.

legs

The most important teaching aspect of the legs is that the action is a series of movements that flow together to make one sweeping leg kicking action.

Heels are drawn up towards the seat. Soles face upwards

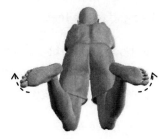

Feet turn outwards to allow the heels and soles to aid propulsion

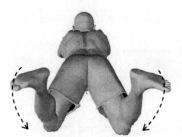

Heels push back and outwards in a whip-like action

It is important for a swimmer or swimming teacher to recognise the difference between the wedge kick and whip kick for breaststroke. The leg action provides the largest amount of propulsion in the stroke and swimmers will favour a wedge kick or a whip kick depending on which comes most naturally. For a whip kick, the legs kick in a whip-like action with the knees remaining close together. For a wedge kick the legs kick in a wider, more deliberate circular path.

The leg kick as a whole should be a simultaneous and flowing action, providing the majority of the propulsion. Knees bend as the heels are drawn up towards the seat and toes are turned out ready for the heels and soles of the feet to drive the water backwards. The legs sweep outwards and downwards in a flowing circular path, accelerating as they kick and return together and straight, providing a streamlined position.

Heels drawn towards the seat and feet turn out

Heels drive back in a circular whip like action giving the kick power and motion

Kick finishes in a streamlined position with legs straight and toes pointed

The amount of propulsion generated from arm techniques has developed over the years as the stroke has changed to become more competitive. The arm action overall provides the smallest propulsive phase of the four competitive strokes.

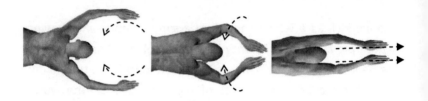

Arms and hands pull around and downwards

Elbows tuck in and arms and hands stretch forward into a glide

Catch

Arm action begins with the arms fully extended out in front, fingers and hands together. Hands pitch outwards and downwards to an angle of about 45 degrees at the start of the catch phase. Arms pull outwards and downwards until they are approximately shoulder width apart. Elbows begin to bend and shoulders roll inwards at the end of the catch phase.

Arms and hands pull back in a circular motion

Propulsive phase

Arms sweep downwards and inwards and the hands pull to their deepest point. Elbows bend to 90 degrees and remain high. At the end of the down sweep, the hands sweep inwards and slightly upwards. Elbows tuck into the sides as the hands are pulled inwards towards the chest and the chin.

Recovery

Hands recover by stretching forwards in a streamlined position. Hands recover under, on or over the water surface, depending on if the style of stroke is competitive or recreational.

breathing

The stroke action contains a natural body lift which gives the ideal breathing point with each stroke.

Inhalation takes place at the end of the in-sweep as the body allows the head to lift clear of the water. The head should be lifted enough for the mouth to clear the surface and inhale, but not excessively so as to keep the frontal resistance created by this movement to a minimum.

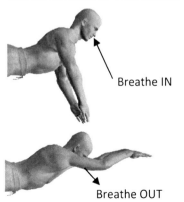

Breathe IN

Breathing in occurs as the arms pull down and the head rises above the surface

Breathe OUT

Breathing out occurs as the arms recover forwards

Explosive or trickle breathing can be utilised.

- Trickle

The breath is slowly exhaled through the mouth and nose into the water during the glide phase. The exhalation is controlled to allow inhalation to take place easily as the arm begins to pull again.

- Explosive

The breath is held after inhalation during the kick and glide phase and then released explosively, part in and part out of the water, as the head is raised to breath.

Head returns to the water to exhale as the arms stretch forward to begin their recovery phase.

Some swimmers perform the stroke with the head raised throughout to keep the mouth and nose clear of the water at all times. This simplifies the breathing but at the expense of overall efficiency. This is also a more recreational method of swimming breaststroke.

timing

The coordination of the propulsive phases should be a continuous alternating action, where one propulsive phase takes over as one ends. The stroke timing can be summed up with the following sequence: pull, breath, kick, glide.

A streamlined body position at the end of that sequence is essential to capitalise on the propulsive phases of the stroke. The timing can be considered in another way: when the arms are pulling in their propulsive phase, the legs are streamlined and when the legs are kicking in propulsion, the arms are streamlined.

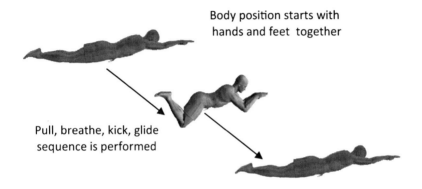

Body position starts with hands and feet together

Pull, breathe, kick, glide sequence is performed

Swimmer returns to original body position.

Full body extension is essential before the start of each stroke cycle.

Competitive variations in stroke timing can be found by decreasing or even eliminating the glide and using the arm and leg actions in an almost continuous stroke to give more propulsion.

full stroke overview

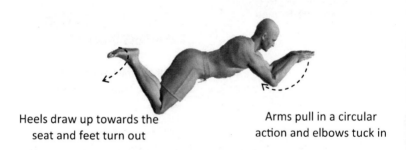

Heels draw up towards the seat and feet turn out

Arms pull in a circular action and elbows tuck in

Arms stretch forward into a glide

Legs kick backwards providing power and propulsion

breaststroke

stroke exercises

The stroke exercises contained in the following part of this book form a reference section for each aspect of breaststroke swimming stroke.

what are they?

Each specific exercise focuses on a certain aspect of the swimming stroke, for example the body position, the leg kick, the arms, the breathing or the timing and coordination, all separated into easy-to-learn stages.   Each one contains a photograph of the exercise being performed, a graphical diagram and all the technique elements and key focus points that are relevant to that particular exercise.

how will they help?

They break down your swimming stroke into its core elements and then force you to focus on that certain area. For example if you are performing a leg kick exercise, the leg kick is isolated and therefore your focus and concentration is only on the legs. The technical information and key focus points then fix your concentration on the most important elements of the leg kick. The result: a more efficient and technically correct leg kick. The same then goes for exercises for the arms, breathing, timing and coordination and so on.

Yes, definitely! These practical exercises not only isolate certain areas but can highlight your bad habits. Once you've worked though each element of the stroke and practiced the exercises a few times, you will slowly eliminate your bad habits. The result: a more efficient and technically correct swimming stroke, swum with less effort!

The page layouts for each exercise follow the same format, keeping all relevant information on an easy-to-follow double page. The aims, technical focuses and key points are all listed with a photograph and graphical diagram of the exercise along with the most common mistakes.

Body Position: Push and glide

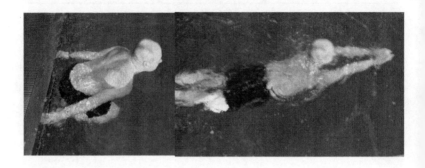

Aim: to develop a basic body position by pushing from the side.

The distance of the glide will be limited due to the resistance created by the chest and shoulders. The exercise can be performed with the face submerged as it would be during the glide phase of the stroke or with the head up facing forwards.

Technical Focus
o Head remains still and central
o Face is up so that only the chin is in the water
o Eyes are looking forwards over the surface
o Shoulders should be level and square
o Hips are slightly below shoulder level
o Legs are in line with the body

Key Actions
o   Push hard from the side
o   Keep head up looking forward
o   Stretch out as far as you can
o   Keep your hands together
o   Keep your feet together

Body position at a slight angle if the head is above the water surface

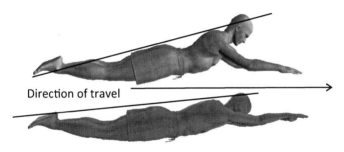

Direction of travel

Body position flatter and more streamlined during the glide phase
when the face is submerged

Common Faults
o   Shoulders and/or hips are not level
o   Head is not central and still
o   One shoulder is in front of the other

Legs: Sitting on the poolside with feet in the water

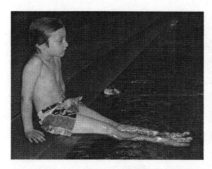 

Aim: to practice the leg action whilst sat stationary on the poolside.

This exercise allows the pupil to copy the teacher who can also be sat on the poolside demonstrating the leg kick. The physical movement can be learnt before attempting the leg kick in the water.

Technical Focus
o   Kick should be simultaneous
o   Legs should be a mirror image
o   Heels are drawn towards the seat
o   The feet turn out just before the kick
o   Feet come together at the end of the kick with legs straight and toes pointed

Key Actions
o Kick your legs simultaneously
o Keep your knees close together
o Kick like a frog
o Make sure your legs are straight and together at the end of the kick

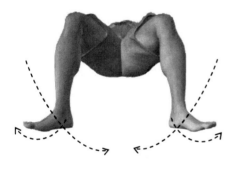

Feet turn out as the legs begin to kick round in a circular action

Common Faults
o Circular kick in the opposite direction
o Only turning one foot out
o Legs are not straight at the end of the kick
o Leg action is not circular

Legs: Supine position with a woggle held under the arms

Aim: to develop breaststroke leg kick in a supine position.

This allows the swimmer to see their own legs kicking. The woggle provides stability for the beginner and, with the swimmer in a supine position, allows the teacher easy communication during the exercise.

Technical Focus
o   Kick should be simultaneous
o   Heels are drawn towards the seat
o   The feet turn out just before the kick
o   Feet kick back with knees just inline with the hips
o   Feet come together at the end of the kick

Key Actions
o   Kick with both legs at the same time
o   Keep your feet in the water
o   Kick like a frog
o   Kick and glide
o   Point your toes at the end of the kick

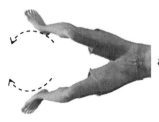

Heels drive back in a circular whip like action giving the kick power and motion

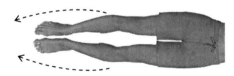

Kick finishes in a streamlined position with legs straight and toes pointed

Common Faults
o   Feet are coming out of the water
o   Failing to bring the heels up to the bottom
o   Leg kick is not simultaneous
o   Legs are not straight at the end of the kick

Legs: Static practice holding the poolside

Aim: to practise breaststroke leg action in a static position.

This allows the swimmer to develop correct technique in a prone position in the water. Kicking WITHOUT force and power should be encouraged during this exercise to avoid undue impact on the lower back.

Technical Focus
o   Legs should be a mirror image
o   Heels are drawn towards the seat
o   The feet turn out just before the kick
o   Feet kick back with knees inline with the hips
o   Feet come together at the end of the kick with legs straight and toes pointed

Key Actions
- o   Kick both legs at the same time
- o   Kick like a frog
- o   Draw a circle with your heels
- o   Make sure your legs are straight at the end of the kick

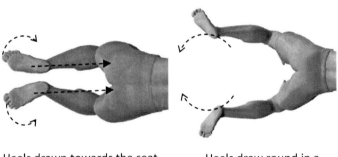

Heels drawn towards the seat and feet turn out

Heels draw round in a circular motion

Common Faults
- o   Only turning one foot out
- o   Legs are not simultaneous
- o   Leg action is not circular

Legs: Prone position with a float held under each arm

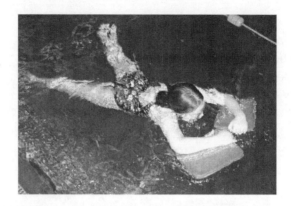

Aim: to practise and develop correct leg kicking technique in a prone position.

Using two floats aids balance and stability and encourages correct body position whilst moving through the water.

Technical Focus
o   Leg kick should be simultaneous
o   Heels are drawn towards the seat
o   The feet turn out just before the kick
o   Feet kick back with knees inline with the hips
o   Feet come together at the end of the kick

Key Actions

o   Keep your knees close together
o   Point your toes to your shins
o   Drive the water backwards with your heels
o   Glide with legs straight at the end of the each kick

Heels are drawn up towards
the seat. Soles face upwards

Heels push back and outwards in
a whip-like action

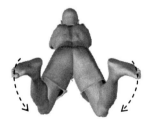

Feet turn outwards to allow the
heels and soles to aid propulsion

Common Faults

o   One foot turns out, causing a 'scissor' like kick
o   Legs kick back and forth
o   Legs kick is not simultaneous
o   Toes are not pointed at the end of the kick

Legs: Holding a float out in front with both hands

Aim: to practise and learn correct leg kicking technique and develop leg strength.

Holding a single float or kickboard out in front isolates the legs and creates a slight resistance which demands a stronger kick with which to maintain momentum.

Technical Focus
o   Kick should be simultaneous
o   Legs drive back to provide momentum
o   Heels are drawn towards the seat
o   The feet turn out before the kick
o   Feet come together at the end of the kick with legs straight and toes pointed

Key Actions

o   Drive the water backwards with force
o   Turn your feet out and drive the water with your heels
o   Kick and glide
o   Kick like a frog
o   Make your feet like a penguin

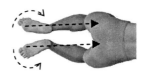

Heels drawn towards the seat and feet turn out

Heels drive back in a circular whip like action giving the kick power and motion

Kick finishes in a streamlined position with legs straight and toes pointed

Common Faults

o   Kick is slow and lacking power
o   Failing to bring the heels up to the bottom
o   Feet are breaking the water surface
o   Toes are not pointed at the end of the kick

Legs: Arms stretched out in front holding a float vertically

Aim: to develop leg kick strength and power.

The float held vertically adds resistance to the movement and requires the swimmer to kick with greater effort. Ideal for swimmers with a weak leg kick.

Technical Focus
o Arms should be straight and float should be held partly underwater
o Kick should be a whip like action
o Feet kick back with knees inline with the hips
o Feet come together at the end of the kick

Key Actions

o Kick your legs simultaneously

o Push the water with your heels and the soles of your feet

o Drive the water backwards with your heels

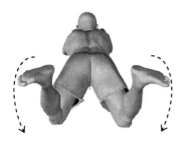

Heels push back and outwards in a whip-like action

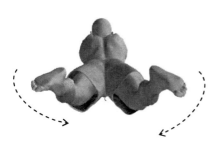

Heels drive back to add power to the kick

Common Faults

o Float is held flat or out of the water

o Not turning both feet out

o Leg kick lacks sufficient power

Legs: Supine position with hands held on hips

Aim: to develop leg kick strength and stamina.

This exercise is more advanced and requires the leg kick to be previously well practised.

Technical Focus
o Kick should be simultaneous
o Heels are drawn towards the seat
o The feet turn out just before the kick
o Feet kick back with knees inline with the hips
o Feet come together at the end of the kick with legs straight and toes pointed

Key Actions
o   Keep your feet in the water
o   Kick like a frog
o   Make sure your legs are straight after each kick
o   Kick and glide
o   Point your toes at the end of the kick

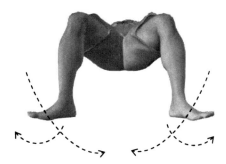

Feet turn out as the legs
begin to kick round in a
circular action

Common Faults
o   Not turning both feet out
o   Kick is not hard enough to provide power
o   Legs are not straight at the end of the kick
o   Toes are not pointed at the end of the kick

Legs: Moving practice with arms stretched out in front

Aim: to practise correct kicking technique and develop leg strength.

This is an advanced exercise as holding the arms out in front demands a stronger kick with which to maintain momentum whilst maintaining a streamlined body position.

Technical Focus
o   Kick should be simultaneous
o   The feet turn out just before the kick
o   Feet kick back with knees just inline with the hips
o   Feet come together at the end of the kick with legs straight and toes pointed

Key Actions

o Keep your knees close together
o Drive the water with your heels
o Make sure your legs are straight at the end of the kick
o Kick and glide

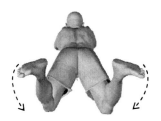

Heels push back and outwards in a whip-like action

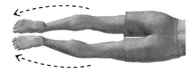

Kick finishes in a streamlined position with legs straight and toes pointed

Common Faults

o Not turning both feet out
o Feet are breaking the water surface
o Legs are not straight at the end of the kick
o Toes are not pointed at the end of the kick

Arms: Static practice standing on the poolside

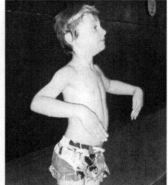

Aim: to learn the arm pull technique in its most basic form.

On the pool side, either sitting or standing, the swimmer can practise and perfect the movement without the resistance of the water.

Technical Focus
o Arm action should be simultaneous
o Fingers should be together
o Arm pull should be circular
o Elbows should be tucked in after each pull
o Arms should extend forward and together after each pull

Key Actions

o Both arms pull at the same time
o Keep your fingers closed together
o Keep your hands flat
o Tuck your elbows into your sides after each pull
o Stretch your arms forward until they are straight
o Draw an upside down heart with your hands

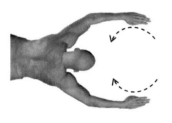 

Arms and hands pull
around and downwards

Elbows tuck in and arms
extend forward

Common Faults

o Fingers apart
o Arms pull at different speeds
o Arms pull past the shoulders
o Elbows fail to tuck in each time
o Arms fail to extend full forward

Arms: Walking practice moving through shallow water

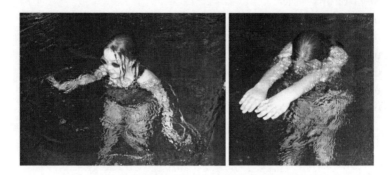

Aim: to practise and develop correct arm technique from in the water.

The swimmer can experience the feel of pulling the water whilst walking along the pool floor. Where the water is too deep, this exercise can be performed standing on the poolside. Submerging the face is optional at this stage.

Technical Focus
o Arm action should be simultaneous
o Arms and hands should remain under water
o Fingers should be together
o Arms should extend forward and together until straight after each pull

Key Actions
o   Pull with both arms at the same time
o   Keep your hands under the water
o   Tuck your elbows into your sides after each pull
o   Stretch your arms forward until they are straight
o   Draw an upside down heart with your hands

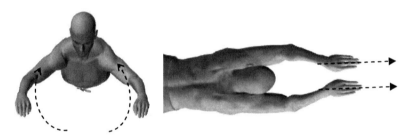

Arms and hands pull back in a   Elbows tuck in and arms and hands
          circular motion   stretch forward into a glide

Common Faults
o   Fingers are apart
o   Arms pull past the shoulders
o   Elbows fail to tuck in each time
o   Arms fail to extend full forward
o   Hands come out of the water

Arms: Moving practice with a woggle held under the arms

Aim: to learn correct arm action whilst moving through the water.

The use of the woggle means that leg kicks are not required to assist motion and this then helps develop strength in the arm pull. The woggle slightly restricts arm action but not enough to negate the benefits of this exercise.

Technical Focus
o Arm action should be simultaneous
o Arms and hands should remain under water
o Arms and hands should extend forward after the pull
o Fingers should be together
o Arm pull should be circular

Key Actions

o Pull round in a circle
o Keep your hands under the water
o Keep your fingers together and hands flat
o Pull your body through the water
o Draw an upside down heart with your hands

Arms and hands pull around
and downwards

Elbows tuck in and arms and hands
stretch forward into a glide

Common Faults

o Fingers are apart
o Arms fail to extend fully forward
o Hands come out of the water
o Arms extend forward too far apart

Arms: Arms only with a pull-buoy held between the legs

Aim: to develop strength in the arm pull.

The pull-buoy prevents the legs from kicking, therefore isolating the arms. As the legs are stationary, forward propulsion and a glide action is difficult and therefore the arm action is made stronger as it has to provide all the propulsion for this exercise.

Technical Focus
o Arms and hands should remain under water
o Arm pull should be circular
o Elbows should be tucked in after each pull
o Arms should extend forward and together

Key Actions

o Keep your hands under the water
o Pull your body through the water
o Keep your elbows high as you pull
o Tuck your elbows into your sides after each pull
o Stretch your arms forward until they are straight

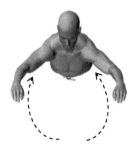

Arms and hands pull back in a
circular motion

Elbows tuck in and arms and hands
stretch forward together

Common Faults

o Arms pull past the shoulders
o Elbows fail to tuck in each time
o Arms fail to extend full forward
o Hands come out of the water
o Arms extend forward too far apart

Arms: Push and glide adding arm pulls

Aim: to progress arm action and technique from previous exercises.

By incorporating a push and glide, this allows the swimmer to practise maintaining a correct body position whilst using the arms. This is a more advanced exercise as the number of arms pulls and distance travelled will vary according to the strength of the swimmer.

Technical Focus
o   Arms and hands should remain under water
o   Elbows should be tucked in after each pull
o   Arms should extend forward into a glide position
o   Body position should be maintained throughout

Key Actions
o Keep your hands under the water
o Pull your body through the water
o Tuck your elbows into your sides after each pull
o Stretch your arms forward with hands together

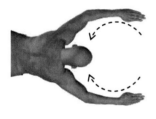

Arms and hands stretch forward
into the original glide position

Arms and hands pull around
and downwards

Common Faults
o Arms pull past the shoulders
o Arms fail to extend full forward
o Hands come out of the water
o Arms extend forward too far apart
o Arms fail to bend during the pull

Breathing: Static practice, breathing with arm action

Aim: to practise breast stroke breathing action whilst standing in the water.

This allows the swimmer to experience the feel of breathing into the water in time with the arm action, without the need to actually swim.

Technical Focus
o   Breath inwards at the end of the in sweep
o   Head lifts up as the arms complete the pull
o   Head should clear the water
o   Head returns to the water as the arms recover
o   Breath out is as the hands recover forward

Key Actions
o Breathe in as you complete your arm pull
o Breathe out as your hands stretch forwards
o Blow your hands forwards

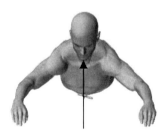

Breathe IN as the arms pull
down and the head rises

Breathe OUT as the arms
recover forward and the face
enters the water

Common Faults
o Head fails to clear the water
o Breathing out as the arms pull back
o Lifting the head to breathe as the arms recover

Breathing: Breathing practice with woggle under the arms

Aim: to develop correct synchronisation of breathing and arm pull technique.

The woggle provides support which enables the exercise to be done slowly at first. It also allows the swimmer to travel during the practice. Leg action can be added if necessary. Note: the woggle can restrict complete arm action.

Technical Focus
o Breath inwards at the end of the in-sweep
o Head lifts up as the arms complete the pull back
o Head should clear the water
o Head returns to the water as the arms recover
o Breathing out is as the hands stretch forward

Key Actions
o Breathe in as you complete your arm pull
o Breathe out as your hands stretch forwards
o Blow your hands forwards

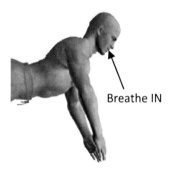

Breathing in occurs as the arms pull down and the head rises above the surface

Breathe IN

Breathing out occurs as the arms recover out in front

Breathe OUT

Common Faults
o Holding the breath
o Head fails to clear the water
o Breathing out as the arms pull back
o Lifting the head as the arms stretch forward

Breathing: Float held in front, breathing with leg kick

Aim: to develop the breathing technique in time with the leg kick.

The float provides stability and allows the swimmer to focus on the breathe kick glide action.

Technical Focus
o   Inward breathing should be just before the knees bend
o   Head lifts up as the knees bend ready to kick
o   Mouth should clear the water
o   Head returns to the water as the legs thrust backwards
o   Breathe out is as the legs kick into a glide

Key Actions
o   Breathe in as your legs bend ready to kick
o   Breathe out as you kick and glide
o   Kick your head down

Breathe IN just before the knees bend for the kick

Breathe OUT as the legs kick into a glide

Common Faults
o   Holding the breath
o   Head fails to clear the water
o   Breathing out as the knees bend ready to kick
o   Lifting the head as the legs kick into a glide

Timing: Slow practice with woggle under the arms

Aim: to practise the stroke timing in its most basic form.

The use of the woggle placed under the arms allows the swimmer to practice the exercise in stages as slowly as they need. It must be noted that the woggle resists against the glide and therefore the emphasis must be placed on the timing of the arms and legs. The glide can be developed using other exercises.

Technical Focus
o From a streamlined position arms should pull first
o Legs should kick into a glide
o Legs should kick as the hands and arms   recover
o A glide should precede the next arm pull

Key Actions

o Pull with your hands first
o Kick your hands forwards
o Kick your body into a glide
o Pull, breathe, kick, glide

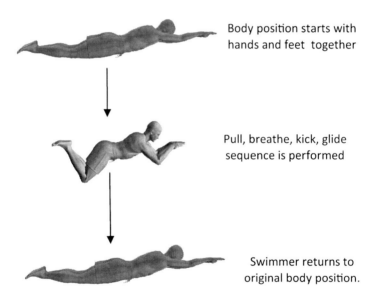

Body position starts with hands and feet together

Pull, breathe, kick, glide sequence is performed

Swimmer returns to original body position.

Common Faults

o Kicking and pulling at the same time
o Failure to glide
o Legs kick whilst gliding

Timing: Push and glide, adding stroke cycles

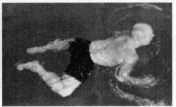

Aim: to practise and develop correct stroke timing.

The swimmer starts with a push and glide to establish a streamlined glide. The arm pull, breath in and then leg kick is executed in the correct sequence, resulting in another streamlined glide.

Technical Focus
o From a streamlined position arms should pull first
o Legs should kick into a glide
o Legs should kick as the hands and arms   recover
o A glide should precede the next arm pull

Key Actions

o   Kick your hands forwards
o   Kick your body into a glide
o   Pull, breathe, kick, glide

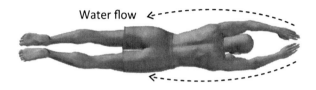

Push and glide to establish body position

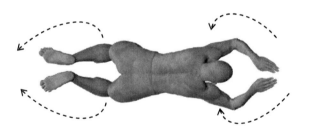

Pull, breathe, kick and glide again

Common Faults

o   Kicking and pulling at the same time
o   Failure to glide
o   Legs kick whilst gliding

Timing: Two kicks, one arm pull

Aim: to perfect timing whilst maintaining a streamlined body position.

From a push and glide, the swimmer performs a 'pull, breathe, kick, glide' stroke cycle into another streamlined glide. They then perform an additional kick whilst keeping the hands and arms stretched out in front. This encourages concentration on timing and coordination and at the same time develops leg kick strength.

Technical Focus
o   Legs should kick into a glide
o   Legs should kick as the hands and arms recover
o   A glide should follow each leg kick
o   Head lifts to breath with each arm pull

Key Actions

o   Kick your body into a glide

o   Pull, breathe, kick, glide

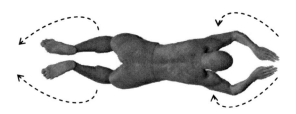

A full stroke cycle is performed from a
push and glide

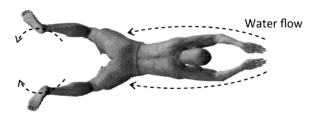

Water flow

Additional kick whilst the hands and arms remain still

Common Faults

o   Arms pull too often and too early

o   Failure to glide

o   Failure to keep the hands together for the second kick

BREASTSTROKE: Full stroke

Aim: to swim full stroke Breaststroke demonstrating efficient arm and leg action, with regular breathing and correct timing.

Technical Focus
o   Head remains still and central
o   Shoulders remain level
o   Leg kick is simultaneous
o   Feet turn out and drive backwards
o   Arm action should be circular and simultaneous
o   Breathing is regular with each stroke cycle

Key Actions
o Kick and glide
o Kick your hands forwards
o Drive your feet backward through the water
o Keep your fingers together and under the water
o Pull in a small circle then stretch forward
o Breath with each stroke

Heels draw up towards the seat and feet turn out

Arms pull in a circular action and elbows tuck in

Legs kick backwards providing power and propulsion

Arms stretch forward into a glide

Common Faults
o Failure to glide
o Stroke is rushed
o Leg kick is not simultaneous
o Arms pull to the sides
o Failing to breath regularly

Breaststroke: Exercise quick reference guide

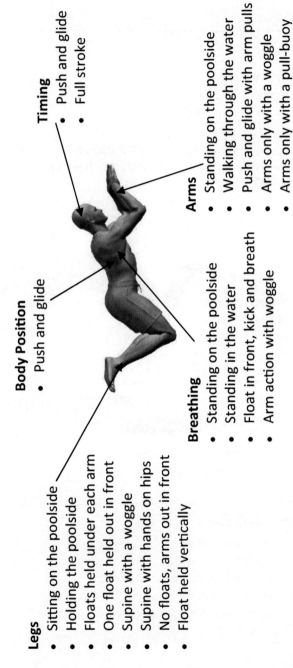

Legs
- Sitting on the poolside
- Holding the poolside
- Floats held under each arm
- One float held out in front
- Supine with a woggle
- Supine with hands on hips
- No floats, arms out in front
- Float held vertically

Body Position
- Push and glide

Breathing
- Standing on the poolside
- Standing in the water
- Float in front, kick and breath
- Arm action with woggle

Timing
- Push and glide
- Full stroke

Arms
- Standing on the poolside
- Walking through the water
- Push and glide with arm pulls
- Arms only with a woggle
- Arms only with a pull-buoy

Index of stroke exercises

The Complete Guide to Swimming Breaststroke
is available in FULL COLOUR as an eBook download

Download it online now from SWIM TEACH
www.swim-teach.com

Also available from all major eBook retailers

For more information about learning to swim and
improving your swimming strokes and swimming
technique visit:

swim-teach.com
www.swim-teach.com

Download Complete Guides to
All Four Basic Swimming Strokes

Lightning Source UK Ltd.
Milton Keynes UK
UKOW041425120712

195876UK00003B/2/P